香港國際詩歌之夜 2013
INTERNATIONAL POETRY NIGHTS IN HONG KONG

編輯 Editors

北島 Bei Dao

陳嘉恩 Shelby K. Y. Chan

方梓勳 Gilbert C. F. Fong

柯夏智 Lucas Klein

馬德松 Christopher Mattison

韓東
Han Dong

目錄 Contents

1 一聲巨響

一聲巨響
我走出去查看
什麼也沒有看見

一小時後
我發現砧板
落在灶臺上
砸碎了一隻杯子

砧板絲紋不動
杯子的碎片也是
靜靜的

當初砧板掛在牆上
杯子在它的下面
也是靜靜的

A Loud Noise

A loud noise
I went out to check
Nothing

An hour later
I discovered the chopping board
Fallen on the cook top
A broken cup

The chopping board lay still
Fragments of the cup were also
Quite quiet

The chopping board used to hang on the wall
The cup beneath it
Both quite quiet

(Translated by Nicky Harman)

2 來自大連的電話

一個來自大連的電話，她也不是
我昔日的情人。沒有目的。電話
僅在敘述自己的號碼。一個女人
讓我回憶起三年前流行的一種容貌

剛剛結婚，在飄滿油漆味兒的新房
正適應和那些莊嚴的家具在一起
（包括一部親自選購的電話）
也許是出於好奇——像年輕的母貓
她在擺弄丈夫財產的同時，意外
撥通了我的電話

大連古老的海浪是否在她的窗前？
是否有一塊當年的礁石仍在堅持
感人的形象？多年以後——不會太久
如果仍有那來自中年的電話，她一定
學會了生活。三十年後
只有波濤，在我的右耳
我甚至聽不見她粗重的海象的呼吸

A Phone Call from Dalian

A phone call from Dalian. It wasn't even
A former lover. It was pointless. The call
Simply gave her phone number. A woman
Made me think back to a type of face popular three
years ago.

She was just married, in a new house smelling of fresh
paint
Which went perfectly with the stately furniture
(Including the phone she'd personally picked)
Was it perhaps just from curiosity (like a young cat)
That, as she fiddled with her husband's possessions, she
happened
To dial my number?

Were Dalian's ancient waves lapping outside her
window?
Was there that rock, still insisting on
Its stirring image? If, many years later—but not too
long

She were to call again, from middle age, she would
  certainly
Have learned about life. Thirty years later
There would just be waves, in my right ear
I would not even hear her harsh, she-animal breathing.

(Translated by Nicky Harman)

3 冬天的荒唐景色

這是冬天的荒唐景色
這是中國的羅馬大街
太陽的鑰匙圈還別在腰上
霞光已打開了白天的門

這是炭條畫出的樹枝
被再次燒成了炭條
這是雪地贈與的白紙
還是畫上雪地

瞧，汽車在表達個性
商店在拍賣自己
梧桐播撒黃葉，一個淮陰人
日夜思念著巴黎

垃圾上升起了狼煙
大廈霧靄般飄移
而人與獸，在爭奪
本屬於獸的毛皮

這是南方的北方寒冬
這是毛巾變硬的室內
這並不是電腦病毒的冬眠期
不過是思之花萎縮的幾日

Absurd Winter Scene

This is an absurd winter scene
This is China's Roman road
The sun's keyring still hangs at the waist
The dawn light opens the door to day

This is a tree branch drawn in charcoal
Then burned once again into a stick of charcoal
This is white paper bestowed by the snowy ground
Lets draw a snowy ground on it

Look, the car expresses individuality
The shop is selling itself off
The plane tree spreads its yellow leaves, someone in
    Willow Village
Dreams of Paris day and night

Smoke signals rise from the rubbish
Tower blocks drift by like a mist
While humans and beasts fight over
Furs which properly belong to the beasts

This is the South's Northern winter cold
This is an indoors where the scarf grows stiff
This is not hibernation time for computer viruses
But it is a few days when the flowers of thought shrivel

(Translated by Nicky Harman)

4 半坡即景

小便池邊，並肩而立
一個說：物是人非
一個說：人是物非
答非所問，爭論未果

一個說：一些女人離開了
一個說：一個哥們死掉了
一個說：我們都還活著
一個說：又換了一茬女人

他們回到樓上繼續喝
剩下的黑方
一個說：何以解憂，惟有杜康
一個說：更有威士忌

Banpo Scene

Standing shoulder to shoulder at the urinals
One says, People ain't what they used to be
The other says, Things ain't what they used to be
A non-sequitur, a pointless argument

One says, Our women have left us
The other says, One of our mates has snuffed it
One says, But we're still alive
The other says, We've got a new bunch of women

They go back upstairs, carry on drinking
The rest of the Black Label
One says, Only Dionysus can assuage our sorrows
The other says, Whisky does it better

(Translated by Nicky Harman)

5 橫渡伶仃洋

對歷史無知者橫渡現實之伶仃洋
會使你暈船，在教科書以外
船尾的飛沫像白孔雀尾巴盛開
曹輝的午飯在他的腹中劇烈地翻滾
而一片白色的藥片讓我的心平靜
中間狀態的人在艙內昏睡
馬達單調的轟鳴外套古老的濤聲
我們的船撫摸著伶仃洋、切開了伶仃洋
浸入其中，漫溢出的海水將兩岸淹沒
從荒涼的海上駛向未來的城
蛇口的樓影像朝陽升起

從珠海到深圳
液體、柔軟的路和移動的墳
有時我們停在它的中間
不離一個地方更遠或者更近
我們擴展了它但無法結束它
在魚和海獸的家裏
並無禮地立於那裏的屋頂
我想到了死，但不是認真的
我的思想更傾向於兩小時以後的宴會

所有暈眩的印象都將被抹掉
只留下「伶仃」二字敲擊著碗盞

此外，我記得特殊環境中與
張文娟小姐惟一的私人接觸——
給了她一枚白色的藥片
但不是遞與床頭我妻子避孕的那枚
（「避暈」而非「避孕」）
她接過，咽得也勉強
因為她的胃正呼應著伶仃洋
不像我那麼敏感，但有
更值得糾正的痛苦表情
她的紅西服也蒙塵、起皺
並手握相當粗的鐵管欄杆進入了底艙
哈，白茫茫的伶仃洋也不是愛情的海洋！

Crossing the Lingdingyang, the Lonely Sea

For those ignorant of history, crossing the real-life
  Lonely Sea
Can make you seasick, outside of textbooks
At the stern, flying foam blooms like a peacock's tail
Cao Hui's lunch lurches violently in his belly
While a white pill calms me
Those in a middling state doze in the cabin
The engine's steady roar cloaks the ancient lapping of
  waves
Our boat is stroking the Lonely Sea, cuts it open
Becomes immersed, the brimming waters swamp both
  shores
From the desolate sea we sail to the coming city
The image of Shekou's buildings rises up like the
  morning sun.

From Zhuhai to Shenzhen
A fluid, supple road and mobile tomb
Sometimes we stop in the middle
Not further from one place or nearer
We've expanded but are unable to end it.

And at the home of fish and water beasts
We stand rudely on their roofs
I've thought about dying, but not that seriously
My thoughts lean more towards the banquet in two
hours' time
Then, all impressions of queasiness will be erased
Leaving only the ding-a-ling sea knocking against the
dishes.

That aside, I remember the special circumstances in
which
I had my only private contact with Miss Zhang
Wenjuan—
I gave her a white pill
Not the contraceptive I pass my wife in bed
(A motion sickness pill, not "the" pill)
She took it, forced herself to swallow
For her stomach, which heaved along with the Lonely
Sea
She seemed less sensitive than me, but wore
A pained expression much more in need of righting

And her red suit was dusty and crumpled.
Then she gripped the crude iron handrail and went below to the cabin
Ha! The white expanse of the Lonely Sea is not the ocean of love!

(Translated by Nicky Harman)

6 在水上

在水上，看見河岸
草又青又黃
一朵白色的白雲
一棵樹和所有的樹
都那麼美
房子不一樣，只有
在這裏才美
我無限嚮往岸上的生活
就像我在岸上
嚮往這條綠水

一條水蛇游了過來，昂著頭
撐船人一篙打在它的七寸上
怎麼可能呢
兩件事都不太可能
午後的河岸像船一樣地運動著
直至落日黃昏
而我在竹排上
像在房子裏一樣地睡著了

From the Water

From the water, I see the river bank
Green and yellow grasses
A white cloud
A tree, and all the trees
Are so beautiful
But the house is different, it's just
Beautiful because it's there
I long for a life on land
Just as, on land
I long for this strip of green water

A water snake swims over, its head erect
Is dealt a killer blow with the punter's paddle
... A likely story!
Two things equally unlikely
The afternoon river bank moving like a boat
Until the sun goes down at dusk
While I, on the bamboo raft
Fall asleep just as I would in a house

(Translated by Nicky Harman)

7 綠樹、紅果

我不在的時候綠樹在那裏
然後我走過去了
然後綠樹的前面還有綠樹
樹杈中間有太陽

我直視著太陽，此刻
它就像紅果
因此整個園子都變成了果園

一些足音紛至沓來
嗡嗡的人聲議論著生活
人影如蟲蠓盤旋、聚集
金星如一滴大大的清涼的眼淚

我仍然在那裏
紅果已經消失
綠樹失色

Green Tree, Red Fruit

The green tree was there before I was
Then I walked past it
Then ahead of the tree, there were more green trees
Between the forked branches was the sun

I looked right at the sun. Just then
It was like a red fruit
And so the whole garden became an orchard

A flurry of footsteps came
A buzzing of voices debated life
People's shadows circled, gathered like gnats
The evening star, a great cool teardrop

I am still there
The red fruit gone
The green trees dulled.

(Translated by Nicky Harman)

8 起霧了

起霧了，或者是煙塵
或者是霧和煙的混合物
沒有人驚訝於這一點

可以直視太陽，在灰白的雲層中
像月亮一樣飄動
沒有人驚訝於這一點

我的這個上午和其他的上午一樣
我的昨天幾乎等於明天
沒有人驚訝於這一點

即使是晴朗的日子我也看不清沿途的花和樹
即使看清了，也記不住
即使記住了，也寫不出

如果我不驚訝於這一點
就沒有人驚訝於這一點

敷衍生活比敷衍一件事容易多了
應付世界也比應付一個人容易多了

增長了即時反應，喪失了全知全能

在一片彌漫的濃霧中我機警地躲避著來往的車輛
穿越這座城

It's Foggy

It's foggy, or smoky
Perhaps it's smog
No one's surprised by that

You can look straight into the sun, floating
Like the moon in ashen clouds
No one's surprised by that

This morning is no different from other mornings
Yesterday and tomorrow are pretty much the same
No one's surprised by that

Even on a clear day I can't see roadside trees and flowers
  clearly
Even if I see them I don't remember them
Even if I remember them I can't write about them

If I'm not surprised by that, then
No one else'll be surprised by that

Easier to muddle through life than to muddle through
one thing
Easier to cope with the world than with one person
More knee-jerk reactions, fewer far-sighted actions

I cut through this fog-blanketed city
Cannily avoiding the traffic

(Translated by Nicky Harman)

9 侍母病

沒有什麼
只是陪她坐著
陪她無所事事
用兩個人的力氣想
要吃飯，要恢復健康

每天都有一場大雨傾盆而下
用她的眼睛看窗外的群山
看激越的閃電
如此明麗
就像在兒童的眼睛裏所見

用我的眼睛看她尖細的骨頭
輕巧猶如小鳥的翅膀
正穿越烏雲
唉，垂暮昏沉的是我
聒噪絕望的是我

At My Mother's Bed-Side

Nothing to do
Except sit with her
Wiling the hours away
Being strong for two, willing her
To eat, to get better

Every day it buckets down with rain
I look at the mountains outside the window with her
  eyes
I see intense lightning
Brilliantly beautiful
As if through a child's eyes

I see with my eyes her sharp bones
Light as a bird's wing
Passing through a dark cloud
Hey, the old dodderer
Ranting in despair—is me.

(Translated by Nicky Harman)

10 老人

老人曾是那麼年輕
精力無限地養育我們
為我們而戰
又為自己的晚景和子女苦鬥
喋喋不休，吵吵嚷嚷
惹人厭煩
突然就像風吹落葉
遮天蔽日的景致已然不再

她的手臂真的就像一截樹枝
比握著的手杖還要乾枯
不為那養育之恩
也不為朝夕相處
只為這衰敗和流失
為這房子裏靜悄悄的沉默
追悔並痛惜

Old Woman

That old woman was young once
She put all her energy into rearing us
Fighting for us
And fighting for her own old age, with her children
She chattered and nagged
Drove us to distraction
Then suddenly like a leaf blown from the tree
That all-pervading presence was gone

Her arms and hands were like twigs
More desiccated than the walking stick she held
It's not because we owe it to her
Nor that she was with us all the time
No, it's this frailty and loss
And this stillness in the room
That makes me deeply sorry

(Translated by Nicky Harman)

11 克服寂寞

我的小狗被關閉在家裏
對門鄰居也養了一條小狗
被關閉在家裏
兩條小狗隔著兩道門從兩邊吠叫
犬聲相聞，偶爾也在樓道見面
雖是男狗女狗但不配對
雖說狐朋狗友，它們並不是狗朋友
彼此之間懷有敵意，也許
敵意比友誼更強烈
更能克服寂寞
結局是對門的那條狗死了，我的小狗
仍吠叫不止
也許虛幻的敵人比現實的敵人
更能克服寂寞

Overcoming Loneliness

My small dog was shut in the flat
The neighbors opposite kept one
Shut in their flat too
The two dogs yapped through the barrier of two doors
They could hear each other, and sometimes met on the landing
They were boy dog and girl dog but didn't mate
We all know dogs like to lay-about in packs, but these two were no pals
You could say hostility was
Stronger than friendship
More help in overcoming loneliness
The end came when their dog died, but my dog
Kept up the yapping
An imaginary enemy may well be better than a real one
At overcoming loneliness.

(Translated by Nicky Harman)

12 一些人不愛說話

一些人不愛說話
既不是啞巴，也不內向
只說必要的話
只是禮節
只浮在說話的上面
一生就這樣過去
寥寥數語即可概括
一些人活著就像墓誌銘
漫長但言詞簡短
像墓碑那樣地佇立著
與我們冷靜相對

Some People Don't Like to Talk

Some people don't like to talk
They're not dumb or introverted
They only speak when necessary
Just courtesies
Just floating on the surface of talk
They spend their whole lives like that
It can be summed up very briefly
The way some people live is like an epitaph
Long years but the words are short and simple
Upright as tomb stones
They stand soberly before us.

(Translated by Nicky Harman)

13 小巷裏

我們走在漆黑的小巷裏
聽見身後的朋友議論説
「他們就像一對夫妻。」
二十年前，確有這樣的可能
她十八，我二十
男才女貌，彼此有意
後來我結婚了
她也嫁人了

如今我已離婚多年
她和老公也分居兩地
但我們之間再也沒有熱望
我在想
無論我們是否曾經共同生活過
走到今天都是一樣的

我和她走在漆黑的小巷裏
就像是對歲月的一個紀念

The Alley

We walked down the alley in the pitch dark
I heard our friends behind us say:
"They're like a married couple."
And, twenty years ago, that might have happened
She was eighteen, I was twenty
We made a fine pair, and fancied each other
Then I married
And so did she.

I've been divorced for years now
And she and her husband are separated too
But there's no rekindling of the warmth between us
I reckon
Whether we ever lived together or not
Makes no difference now.

She and I, walking down the alley in the pitch dark,
A memento of those times.

(Translated by Nicky Harman)

14 賣雞的

他擁有迅速殺雞的技藝，因此
成了一個賣雞的，這樣
他就不需要殺人，即使在心裏
他的生活平靜溫馨，從不打老婆
脱去老婆的衣服就像給雞褪毛
相似的技藝總有相同之處
殘暴與溫柔也總是此消彼長
當他脱雞毛、他老婆慢騰騰地收錢的時候
我總覺得這裏面有某種罪惡的甜蜜

The Chicken-Seller

He's got the knack for killing chickens quick, so
He became a chicken-seller, that way
He doesn't need to kill people. Even though he acts
Calm and gentle, and never beats his wife
Taking off his wife's clothes is like plucking a chicken
Similar skills always overlap, just as
Cruelty and kindness are two sides of the same coin
He plucks, and she leisurely takes the money
And I feel that therein lies a kind of evil sweetness

(Translated by Nicky Harman)

15 老樓吟

一棟灰暗的老樓
人們上上下下
進出於不同的門戶
接近頂層時大多消失不見
居於此地三十年
鄰人互不相識
人情涼薄，更是歲月滄桑
孩子長大，老人失蹤
中年垂垂老矣
在樓道挪步
更有新來者，面孔愈加飄忽
老樓的光線愈加昏黃
燈泡不亮，窗有蛛網
雜物橫陳，播撒虛實陰影
人們穿梭其間，一如當年
有提菜籃子的，有拎皮箱的
有互相挎著吊著摟摟抱抱的
更有追逐嬉鬧像小耗子的
有真的耗子如狗大小
真的狗站起比人還高
一概上上下下

七上八下
一時間又都消失不見
鑰匙嘩啦，鋼門哐啷
回家進洞也
惟余無名老樓，搖搖不墮
如大夢者

Dirge of the Old Building

In a gloomy old block of flats
People go up and down
In and out of different doors
As they get near the top floor, most disappear
People who've lived here thirty years
Scarcely know each other
They're meagre with their feelings—times have been so turbulent
Children grow up, the elderly go missing
The middle-aged sink into old age
Footsteps move along the corridor
Especially with newcomers, faces are ever more elusive
The lighting in the block of flats ever dimmer
Bulbs don't work, cobwebs cover windows
There's a scattering of junk, of shifting shadows
People shuttle between them, just like back then …
Carry shopping baskets, lug leather suitcases
Some hang round each other's necks, in each other's arms
More go in search of fun, like rats
There are real rats as big as dogs

There are real dogs that stand taller than a human
Up and down, up and down they go
It's pandemonium
All at once, they've vanished from our view
With a scrape of the key, a clang of the iron door
Getting home is retreating to a cave
All that remains is a nameless old block of flats,
  staggering along
Like a great sleep-walker.

(Translated by Nicky Harman)

16 工人的手

他懸掛在高樓上
抓著牆壁的手紋絲不動
我覺得是女人就應該愛上這隻手
就應該接受它的撫摩
是男人就應該有這樣的手
結實、骯髒，像肉墊吸盤
是女人就應該做那面牆
降低一些吧
最好躺下
是男人就應該死死地抓住那女人
渾身大汗淋漓，但手不出汗
心不跳，腿也不抖
如果是個戀物癖就這樣戀吧
工人的手也是最棒的工具

The Worker's Hand

He hangs suspended from the building
The hand that grips the wall is motionless
A woman should fall in love with that hand
Should receive its caresses
A man should have a hand like this
Strong, grimy, like a fleshy sucker pad
A woman should be that wall
Drop down a bit, or better still,
Lie down
A man should hold that woman in a vice-like grip
His body soaked in sweat (but not his hand
No leaping heart or quivering legs)
If this is fetishism, then lets love this way!
The worker's hand is a marvelous tool

(Translated by Nicky Harman)

17 這些年

這些年，我過得不錯
只是愛，不再戀愛
只是睡，不再和女人睡
只是寫，不再詩歌
我經常罵人，但不翻臉
經常在南京，偶爾也去
外地走走
我仍然活著，但不想長壽

這些年，我缺錢，但不想掙錢
缺覺，但不吃安定
缺肉，但不吃雞腿
頭禿了，那就讓它禿著吧
牙蛀空了，就讓它空著吧
剩下的已經夠用
鬍子白了，下面的鬍子也白了
眉毛長了，鼻毛也長了

這些年，我去過一次上海
但不覺得上海的變化很大
去過一次草原，也不覺得

天人合一
我讀書，只讀一本，但讀了七遍
聽音樂，只聽一張CD，每天都聽
字和詞不再折磨我
我也不再折磨語言

這些年，一個朋友死了
但我覺得他仍然活著
一個朋友已邁入不朽
那就拜拜，就此別過
我仍然是韓東，人稱老韓
老韓身體健康，每周爬山
既不極目遠眺，也不野合
就這麼從半山腰下來了

These Past Few Years

I've not done badly these past few years
Except that I love but have no more love affairs
And sleep, but not with women any more
And though I write, there's no more poetry
I'm often surly, but don't fall out with anyone
I'm usually in Nanjing, though there's an off-chance
I might go out of town on trips
I'm alive, but not looking forward to old age

These past few years, I've been short of money but have
  no desire to earn
I'm short of sleep, but not on tranqs
Short of meat, but I don't eat chicken legs
I'm going bald—hey, let the hairs fall out
I'm losing teeth—well, so be it
I can get by with the ones I've got left
My beard's gone grey—and so's my "beard" down there
Long hairs grow from my eyebrows, and out of my
  nostrils

These past few years, I've been to Shanghai once

But I didn't see those "great changes"
I've been once to the grasslands, but I didn't feel
"At one with Nature"
I've read books—or rather one book, seven times
Listened to music, just one CD, the same one every
  day
Words don't torment me any more
And I don't torment language either.

These past few years, a friend has died
But it still feels like he's alive
Another's shot to fame
So it's bye-bye. Let's part right here
I'm still Han Dong but now they call me "old man"
This old man's still hale, goes hiking every week
Though he doesn't gaze from the hilltop, or have sex
  outdoors any more
And half-way up the hill, he's on his way down again

(Translated by Nicky Harman)

18 小姐

她的衣服從來不換
我注意到，它是美麗、骯髒的
它是表姐的
窮人無二件

我注意到她身處的店堂、我們分屬的階級
而性的微塵無理智地來往
裸體的必要，比穿衣打扮更簡單
服飾比身體更令人羞愧，是可能的

「小姐，你的窮
是空缺的財富
你的空虛很實在，臉蛋兒被油膩襯托得更美。」

她的青春在搬動桌椅中度過一年

Waitress

She's never changed her clothes
I notice they're pretty, and dirty
They belong to her cousin
The poor don't have a change of clothes.

I notice the shop she's in, our class difference,
Dust specks of sex, irrational, move between us.
The need for nakedness, much simpler than dressing
up.
A fine outfit is far more shaming than a body, possibly.

"Miss, your poverty
Is a wealth of vacancy.
Your emptiness quite material, your face made lovelier
by contrast with the grease."

A year of her youth has passed in moving chairs and
tables

(Translated by Nicky Harman)

19 走走看看

去下面走一走
去附近看一看
辦一點瑣碎小事
看一片遼闊風景

看一看那些樹
看一看頭上的天
看城市道路四通八達
車輛暢行無阻

看一看人，看一看狗
看一看人溜狗
看人穿衣很正常
狗穿衣就不一樣

看一看商店
琳琅滿目
看一看書店
讓寫書的我絕望

看一看摩天樓
看一看立交橋
看一看工地和兒童
死的活的都在長

趁某根神經還在
多看幾眼姑娘吧
願時光永駐
色香味俱佳

去下面走一走
去附近看一看
最後盯住手錶一通猛看
幻景頓時煙消雲散

Walking and Looking

Go down, take a walk
Go around, take a look
Get a few things done
Look at the vast cityscape

Take a look at those trees
Take a look at the sky
Look at the city criss-crossed with streets
Vehicles racing along them

Take a look at people, take a look at dogs
Take a look at people walking their dogs
People wearing clothes, that's normal
Dogs wearing clothes, that's quite different

Take a look at shops
A feast for the eyes
Take a look at bookshops
As a writer they make me despair

Take a look at skyscrapers
Take a look at flyovers
Take a look at construction sites and kids
Alive and dead, all growing

If there's a nerve left in your body
Take a few more looks at girls
I want time to stand still
It looks, tastes and smells perfect

Go down, take a walk
Go around, take a look
Finally, stare fiercely at your watch
The illusion's gone in an instant

(Translated by Nicky Harman)

20 我們坐在街上

我們坐在街上
店鋪裏的燈光熄滅了
天色將明未明之際
青色的帷幕下面
對面的黑影僵硬

一年沒見
但已經無話可說
火熱的鍋冷了
酒寒像心情
開始的清晨在熬夜的人看來
像慘淡的結局

We Sat on the Street

We sat on the street
The shop lights were switched off
A crack of dawn in the night sky
The shadow opposite was rigid
Beneath the blue-black curtain

We hadn't seen each other for a year
But there was nothing left to say
The pot had gone off the boil
Liquor chills like feelings cool
If you've been up all night, the start of a new day
Is like a dreary ending

(Translated by Nicky Harman)

21 報紙

一個退休的老頭發誓
要把報紙上的每一個字
都讀到
已經不可能了

報紙鋪天蓋地
中華紙賤
便宜了撿廢紙的老太

難怪一個職業殺手
關在房子裏
不看報十年如一日
培養殺氣

這事兒我也是在報紙上讀到的

Newspaper

A pensioner swears
That reading
Every word of the newspapers
Is impossible nowadays

Newspapers are ubiquitous
Chinese paper so dirt cheap
It cheapens the old litter-picker woman

No wonder a professional killer
Shut himself in the house
Ten years flashed by, he didn't read a newspaper,
Cultivated a murderous energy

I read that in the newspaper too.

(Translated by Nicky Harman)

韓東，1961年5月17日生，1982年畢業於山東大學哲學系。詩人、小說家、劇作家。

著有詩集《白色的石頭》、《爸爸在天上看我》、《重新做人》；中、短篇小說集《我們的身體》、《我的柏拉圖》、《明亮的疤痕》、《美元硬過人民幣》、《此呆已死》；長篇小說《扎根》、《我和你》、《小城好漢之英特邁往》、《知青變形記》、《中國情人》；電影劇本《在清朝》、《北京時間》、《愛你一萬年》等。2012年他出版了雙語詩集《來自大連的電話》。

曾獲「劉麗安詩歌獎」、「華語文學傳媒大獎長篇小說獎」、「高黎貢文學節主席獎」、「金陵文學大獎」，以及「曼氏亞洲文學獎」提名。

Han Dong was born in 1961, and graduated in philosophy from Shandong University in 1982. He is a poet, novelist and screenwriter.

His chief works include the poetry collections *White Stones* (《白色的石頭》), *Dad's Looking Down on Me from the Sky* (《爸爸在天上看我》), and *Becoming a New Person* (《重新做人》); the short story and novella collections *Our Bodies* (《我們的身體》), *My Plato* (《我的柏拉圖》), *Bright Scars* (《明亮的疤痕》), *The Dollar Beats the RMB* (《美元硬過人民幣》), and *This Moron is Dead* (《此呆已死》); the novels *Striking Root* (《扎根》, translated as *Banished!*, published by the University of Hawai'i Press), *Me and You* (《我和你》), *A Small Town Hero Strides out* (《小城好漢之英特邁往》), *Metamorphosis of an Educated Youth* (《知青變形記》), and *A Chinese Lover* (《中國情人》); the screenplays *A Touch of Sin* (《在清朝》), *Beijing Days* (《北京時間》), and *I'll Love You Forever* (《愛你一萬年》). A bilingual volume of his poems, *A Phone Call from Dalian* (《來自大連的電話》), was published by The Chinese University Press and Zephyr Press in 2012.

Han Dong has won the Liu Li'an Poetry Prize, the Chinese Language Media Prize for Novels, the Gao Li Gong Literary Festival Chairman's Prize, and the Jin Ling Literary Prize. 《扎根》(*Banished!*) was longlisted for the Man Asian Literary Prize.

出版 Publisher
香港中文大學出版社 The Chinese University Press

封面影像 Cover Image
北島 Bei Dao

出版日期 Date of Publication
二零一三年十一月 November 2013

國際書號 ISBN
978-962-996-626-3

香港國際詩歌之夜 2013 International Poetry Nights in Hong Kong 2013
主辦單位 Organizers
香港中文大學文學院 Faculty of Arts, The Chinese University of Hong Kong
香港浸會大學文學院 Faculty of Arts, Hong Kong Baptist University
香港科技大學人文社會科學學院 School of Humanities and Social Science, The Hong Kong University of Science and Technology

合作夥伴 In Partnership With
英國文化協會 British Council

協辦單位 Co-organizers
時刻文化 Moment Communications
香港中文大學出版社 The Chinese University Press

贊助 Sponsors
香港兆基創意書院 HKICC Lee Shau Kee School of Creativity
中國會 The China Club
周凱旋基金會 Chau Hoi Shuen Foundation

Printed in Hong Kong